BIPOLAR PSYCHOSIS AND ME

Table of Contents

Chapter 1: What Bipolarity means to me

I am not Bipolar, bipolar is me
Now do you see semantics is key?
I say I am Bipolar: now I have a condition
I say Bipolar is the way I see, and finally, you listen

My journey to the edge of sanity was filled with grief and humanity
Only now in my humility, can I tell you what happened to me
Without pretension, let's explore intervention
From diagnosed and lost, to living with intention

I was a right mess - gave my sister a fright
Banging on her door, in the middle of the night
4am, if I recall... In my head, nothing at all
But just one thought, and one thought only:
'She cannot breathe!!! I need to hurry!!'

So bang bang bang, fists in a flurry
I hurt my hands in my worry

She opened the door, face warped in confusion
"What's going on?"
I charge in, no hesitation

I strip off my clothes, I say I am pregnant
I'm about to give 'birth' at any second
She calms me down I ask for 'air katira'
The sweetened beverage She'd offered me earlier

I cannot stop talking, my mouth runs away
My thoughts are on fire, I'm struggling to stay
Focused and calm, She calls us a cab
She guides me along I'm lost and I'm mad

I ask to collect a roach on the floor, to put in her bag, I really implored
I've gone without sleep For 4 days or more
It was starting to project And could not be ignored

And now at the end, at the car ride's conclusion
I was admitted into a mental health institution

I stood by the pond watching the fish
Oh, how they were still , I did this
I stopped the movement within the water
For I am God, and I have the power
Power to make the fish swim or go

Nobody stop me, watch as I control
The rain and thunder, here I am
The one true messiah of my motherland

So this set the course of my very first admission
I guess it was the start of my now life-long mission

To live as authentically as I can,
I know I'm not God, I am but only man
But that was the me in my lofty confusion
God was so real, in all my delusions

Us at the hospital - sweet, sweet reunion
Me, an agnostic, praying in unison
With those who had faith, I prostrated on the floor
There must be a reason I was called here for..?

The days would pass and I'd miss my daughter
I was warded in 3 different places altogether
An isolation unit, when I was having a fever
An all-female ward, and the Mood Disorders keeper

I danced to the songs on the radio

I peed on the floor, clear through my clothes
I tried to take a joy-ride in an old woman's wheelchair
Believed my blue hair dye was diseased hair

A couple of times, I recall the restraints
Tied to a chair, bound to the bed
I wasn't a danger unto myself...
Or maybe I was, but I couldn't know that

The nurses had to keep me in diapers
And twice a day they'd give me showers
I really enjoyed the pampering and care
Even if I wasn't really mentally all there

When after my sanity started trickling in,
They stopped tying me up, and I started to sing:
To pass the time, to cheer my new friends
To brighten the ward: patient, staff; and mend

I made some good friends at the mood disorders unit
Plenty of writers and poets and wouldn't you know it?
The crazy ones are always the same: Moved by a force called the creative brain
No stranger to chaos, we decay in the mundane

The four walls of IMH designed to contain,
Protect and service an ailing, poorly mind
But the heart is a flower that needs constant sunshine

So I tried to be that breath of fresh air
With my voice, singing here, singing there

For a while, that strategy worked I was relatively happy, until I awoke
I missed my daughter dearly, I had to go home
IMH will always be a haven, bespoke

BUT if I could change a thing or two
I'd do away with the sugary food
The tea-time cakes and raisin bread
Oh how much did I pack on the weight!

Now hard to lose, the kilos I put on
And too, memories of faces with all their hope, gone
The effects of medication: an empty, blank stare
Even if it was a dream, I wouldn't go back there

<u>**Chapter 6: At home, again**</u>

At home at last, I had my freedom
But it was not to be…
For nary a few days passed before I was back at MDU, Ward C

I went to the park, I took a short walk, and sat down in the rain
A builder walked past and laughed at the sight of a fully-dressed insane
He held an umbrella and looked at me, quizzically
I smiled and continued my little game

I was just having fun feeling the rain, not the sun
I had no qualms and no shame
Dancing in the mud, playing in the sand
I did what naturally came

Let's stop to think:
If a child were to do this, would you even think twice?
Is it not the way of children to live in the moment
And to the heart, comply?

But as an adult, a fully grown woman
I was not allowed to play
I was lost in the moment, fully myself
But the decision was made to send me back to 'health'

<u>**Chapter 7: Readmission**</u>

So back I went to my place of imprisonment
I was sent to repent, for being indecent
All I wanted, really, was to play
But somehow I broke some kind of law that day

I was fully in charge of my actions and voice,
This was not me unaware of my choice

But executive decisions were now out of my control
Because I could not comply with the traditional role
Of sane adult, with no compulsion
To play in the rain and dance in fountains

So really, the lesson I learned was to be
Less of a child, less me, less free

Ask any doctor , they'll tell you it's wrong
To yell in the wards, or burst out in song

Time, place and measure, something I've learned
Do what you want, but you must discern
How people react, how they will receive
Your apparent psychosis puts them at ill-ease

The doctors were right, I needed to listen
To have my condition be in remission
I took all the drugs, I had all my jabs
The only real problem was, I couldn't be sad

I became numb, my heart could not grieve
Everyday was about living to breathe
To hug my daughter, I did not feel love
I just felt tired, and cold to my nerves

I needed the warmth, if I wanted to live
This empty, vacant heart could no longer give
I'll take an aching heart, any day
Melancholy and sadness to take with the gay

I live now with balance - to find and maintain
What is mania but creative change?
Yes, what is depression but introspection?
I learned to watch, then control flow's direction

Control is the factor between madness and play
One needs the doctors, the other is okay

A good doctor can help you set limits
Your soul is boundless - your fire is lit
Stoke it high and it might burn you, keep it calm and it can serve you

And if ever you find your fire's died, remember that tomorrow's sunrise
Brings with it a brand new flare. Borrow sunshine, but use care

<u>**Chapter 9: Manic Depression**</u>

Mania and depression come and go on the wind
The line between harmony and chaos is but thin

To wit, my heart cannot take another round of drugs
To numb the grief and humanity, and freeze the function: love

So help me as I am, I wish to take a stand:
Perhaps the way to healing is for man to become friend

With all his inner workings, the child he left behind
If children learned to dance and sing, would it not be a crime

To take away their voices and say 'sit down and shut it'
And call that resolution: 'Mental illness, solved it'

I mean to say confusion, when treated as contusion
Will only hurt the process of human being human

NUTRITIONAL PSYCHIATRY:
Food as your Brain's Medicine

Table of Contents

So here I am, back again
Back at writing, with my faultily-wired brain

They put me on Abilify
So far so good, I still can cry

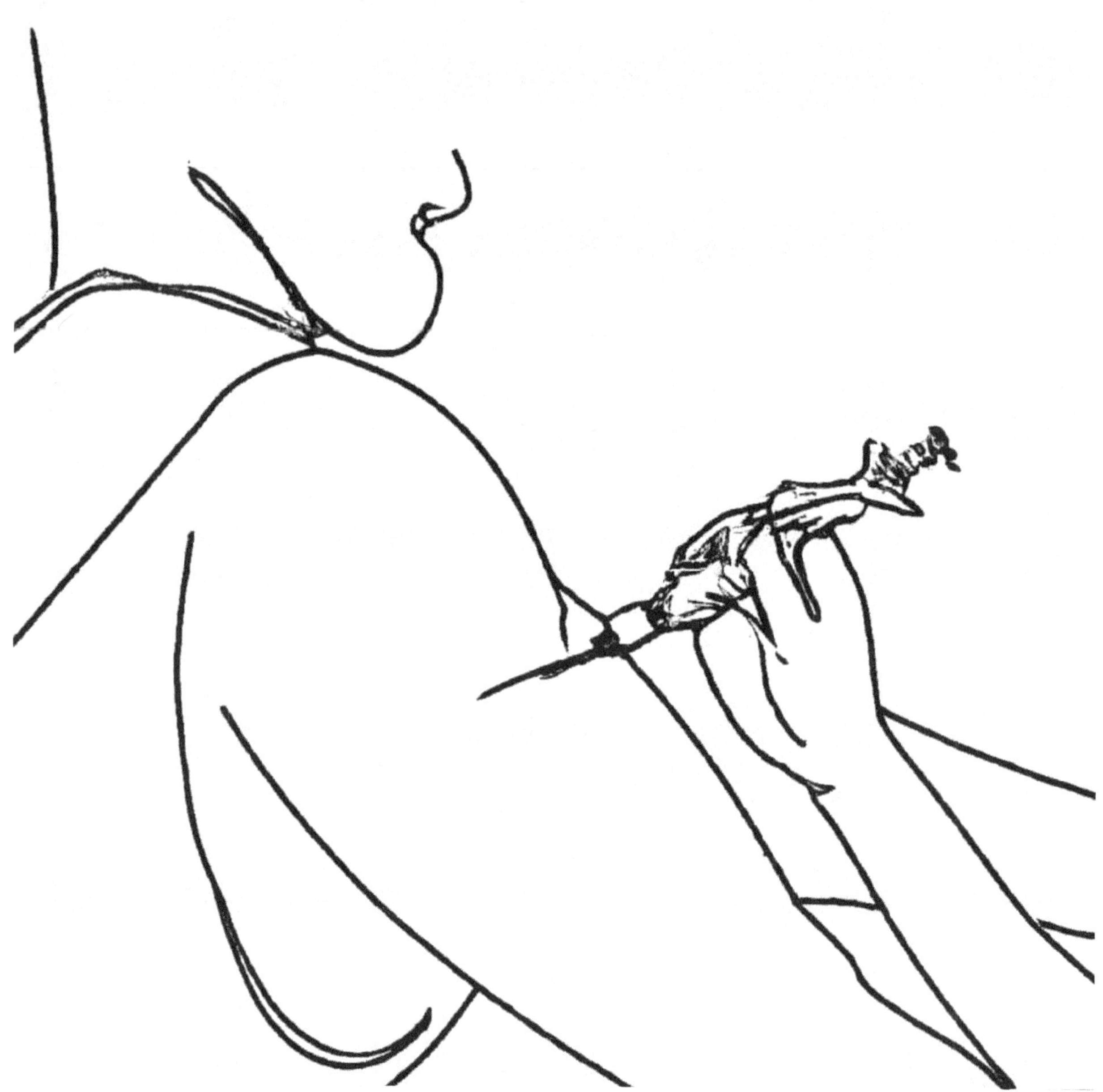

My mind doesn't wander, soar or race
I appear normal, my illness almost has no trace

But only I know what it means to be on medication
One day, the side effects will catch up, and I'll be unwell, all messed up

I worry about the tics, the involuntary movements
How can knowing I will get sick be any improvement?

Chapter 11: **Writing spell**

So I write, under a spell
I can't stop writing, I'm almost in hell

The words just keep coming, although it's not half bad
At least I'm productive, and for that I'm glad

But how far will I go, this manic episode
Will I find myself back in my IMH abode?

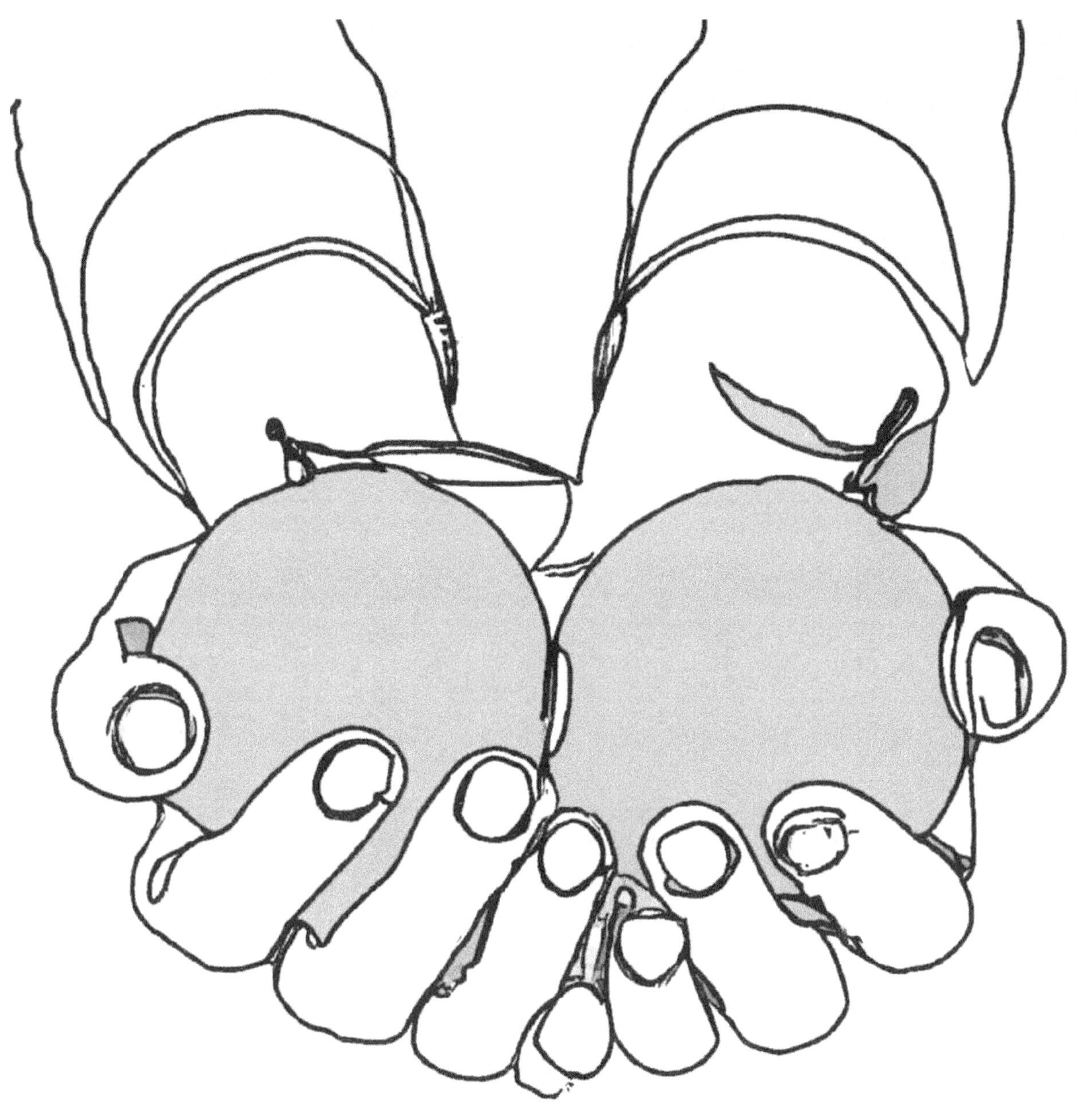

Chapter 12: **Chinese New year**

It's Chinese New year, we all get together
To celebrate family, one day of every year

My parents have made it very clear
I don't need medication - now, I am all ears

They say (and there is support for this) that food is your medicine or poison
I'm currently studying the effects of what I consume, in what proportion

Eating junk food inflames the brain, so maybe therein lies the fault and blame

I have not been taking good care of myself
It's no wonder then, that I am in such poor health

Chapter 13: **Priming myself up for discourse**

Today marks the day I start eating cleaner
Less processed and treated, so I can be leaner

There's much to be learned, I'm taking a course
On nutrition and the body, so I'll be ready for discourse

I am a work in progress
The goal is to get my BMI down, fast

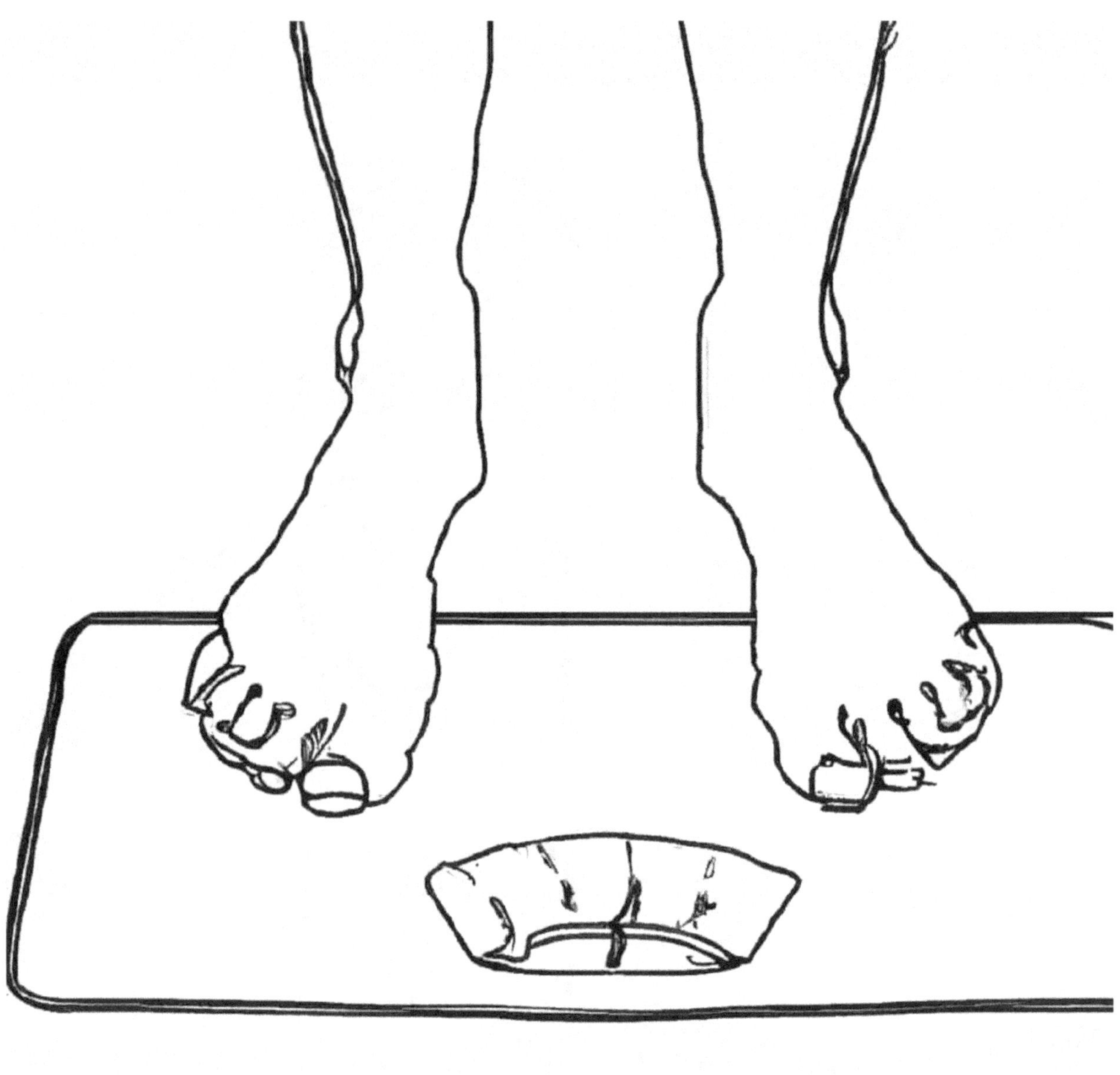

Right now I stand at 115 kilos
I'm not on any diet, not Atkins, not keto

My ideal, healthy weight for my height of 170cm
Is 65kg, and not one more milligram

It won't be easy, but it's not too hard

To eat more nutritiously, because I'm inspired

It's no pain to give up the chemicals
Making me sick, It is not regrettable

I just want to get better and feel good
So I'll stay the course and eat what I should

I know what drove me mad
And for a long time, made me sad

I experienced birth trauma with my firstborn
She was taken away, leaving me forlorn

Under the harsh lights of the hospital, lying on the bed
I was guided by the head when instinct should have led

First, the midwife pressed down hard on my belly

And screamed at me to 'push', repeatedly

Apparently I was doing so bad
I just lay there eventually and said 'leave me and my baby for dead'

And when she was finally out of my cavity
They took her away, which messed with my sanity

I know they had to take her for blood tests immediately
But nothing could assuage the animal instinct built into me

Chapter 16: **Breastfeeding and Medication**

Still I tried to breastfeed as best as I could
For 11 months I succeeded, all well and good

But when I didn't sleep for 4 days straight
I entered into psychosis, a temporary state

For this condition I was medicated for life
They gave me antipsychotics, which came with a price

I could no longer grieve or feel love for my children

Their crying destroyed me, their hugs just felt alien

The drugs also came with horrible, debilitating side effects
My eyes would roll up at random, giving me no time to react

I could be crossing a busy intersection
When my body would decide to have this reaction

It was dangerous for my mind, body and soul
To treat with medication the psychological

I'm not saying the drugs didn't work
But at what cost, what price is your mental health worth?

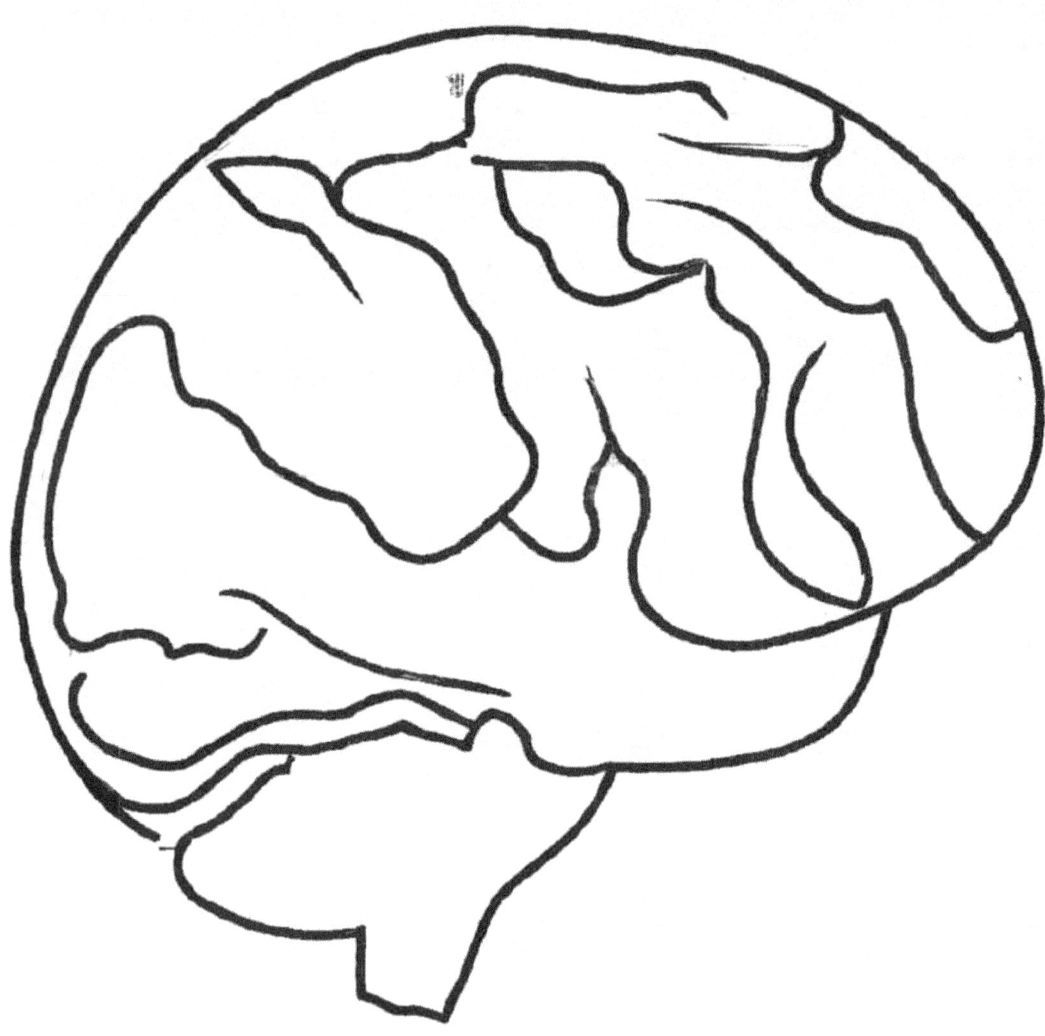

Although the brain only accounts for 2% of our body weight
It requires 20-40% of the glucose and nutrients that we consume in our diet

In order to make sure our brain is functioning as well as can be,
We need to make sure we are feeding it what it needs

Ultra-processed foods are easily accessible ready to eat and often cheap and available
However, these foods have only been around at best for the past century

There is now growing evidence that these foods are harming both our physical and our
mental health, along with a lifestyle that's sedentary

- Excerpted and modified from Edx's Mental Health and Nutrition course by
  University of Canterbury

Chapter 18: **In conclusion**

There is a gap in information regarding recovery
Science is a process of endless discovery

As Einstein once said, 'no amount of experimentation can ever prove me right;
a single experiment can prove me wrong'

I'd like to think, although the road ahead is long
There are many others on this path, journeying along

Perhaps one day we'll change the narrative

I know all our stories are imperative

To the changing landscape that is understanding humanity
The first step is allowing people to embrace their spirituality/insanity

About the Author

Shermin Lee was born in 1993 in the little red dot, Singapore. From a young age, she showed a keen interest in the arts, often spending hours writing poetry and singing. As she grew older, Shermin pursued her passion for the arts, earning a diploma in Mass Communication from Ngee Ann Polytechnic. She worked as an emcee and performer, sharing her love of communication and music with her audiences.

In 2016, Shermin became pregnant with her first child. The birth of her daughter was traumatic, and she struggled with postpartum depression in the year that followed. Unaware that her mental and emotional health were imbalanced, Shermin found it difficult to manage her symptoms, and in 2017, she was diagnosed with bipolar disorder.

Determined to find holistic approaches to healing, Shermin began to explore alternative therapies and lifestyle changes. She adopted a diet rich in whole foods, incorporating plenty of fruits, vegetables, and healthy fats. She also began to prioritize exercise, spending time outdoors and engaging in activities such as walking and dancing. To manage her bipolar symptoms, Shermin discovered the benefits of natural sunlight and began spending time outside each day.

As she continued her journey towards holistic healing, Shermin also turned to her creative passions. She found that during her manic episodes, she was able to channel her energy into her art and music, producing some of her most powerful and evocative work. During her depressive episodes, Shermin turned to deep rest and self-care, using techniques such as listening to music and writing, to manage her symptoms. She incorporates humming, whistling and singing into her daily practice, writes poetry and plays music on her flow days. She rests on her ebb days.

Today, Shermin is the proud mother of two children and continues to pursue her passions for art and music. She has found a sense of peace and balance in her life through her holistic approach to healing and remains committed to sharing her experiences and knowledge with others who may be struggling with bipolar disorder.

Visit *amazon.com/author/sherminlee* for more books like the one you just read.

www.ingramcontent.com/pod-product-compliance
Lightning Source LLC
Chambersburg PA
CBHW081025260726
48662CB00026B/3155